John Hogarth Lozier

40 Rounds from the Cartridge Box of the fighting Chaplain

John Hogarth Lozier

40 Rounds from the Cartridge Box of the fighting Chaplain

ISBN/EAN: 9783337148898

Printed in Europe, USA, Canada, Australia, Japan

Cover: Foto ©ninafisch / pixelio.de

More available books at **www.hansebooks.com**

"Forty Rounds"

From the Fighting Chaplain

INCLUDING

"RHYMES OF TENDERFOOT AND GRAYBACK TIMES,"

AND ALL THE OLD

WAR SONGS

MOST POPULAR IN CAMP-FIRES AND RE-UNIONS;

TOGETHER WITH ALL THE CHOICE RECITATIONS USED IN THE ENTERTAINMENTS

OF

CHAPLAIN LOZIER.

PRICE, 25 CENTS.

ENTERTAINMENTS

For the Benefit of Posts of the G. A. R., and the Women's Relief Corps, and Sons of Veterans.

CHAPLAIN LOZIER

Will give one or more entertainments for the above purpose, on terms that he will *guarantee* will prove a *benefit* to any Post or other organization that sends for him. His entertainments consist of his own unique and captivating Speeches and Recitations, interspersed with his own songs and the best old War Songs extant, Tableaux, etc., etc. One evidence of the captivating character of the Chaplain's entertainments is the fact that wherever he has gone they have immediately requested his return; and in nearly every case he has returned the second night to be greeted by largely increased crowds. His entertainment is entitled

"A Night With the 'Fighting Chaplain.'"

Whoever desires him should write *soon*, so that they may get upon his list in time.

For circulars and all particulars, address (with stamp)

J. H. LOZIER,

DEPARTMENT CHAPLAIN, G. A. R.,

MT. VERNON, - - IOWA.

40

ROUNDS

FROM THE CARTRIDGE BOX OF THE

Fighting Chaplain

EMBRACING THE "CREAM" OF THE "OLD WAR SONGS" AND RECITATIONS, AND THE ODES OF THE

W. R. C.

G. A. R.   S. of V.

PRICE   25 CTS

Per Dozen to Posts, Camps, Corps or Agents, at the rate of 15 Cents Each, Post Paid.

The "Old Soldiers'" Auld Lang Syne.

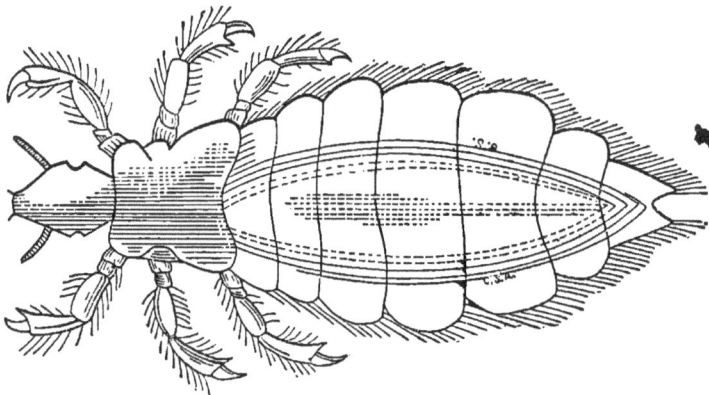

Should Auld Acquaintance be Forgot

And Never
Brought

TO MIND?

Should we forget the "Boys" we met
In the days of auld lang syne?
CHORUS.—For auld lang syne, my "Boys,"
For auld lang syne,
We'll take a cup o' coffee yet
For auld lang syne.

We twa ha'e dodged among the trees
And pu'd the chickens fine;
But we've wandered mony a weary foot
Sin' auld lang syne!—CHORUS.

We're limping lamely down the hill
To life's last "picket line,"
But our old hearts beat warmly still
For auld ald syne!—CHORUS.

From the Cedar Rapids Gazette, June 1st, 1886.

THE FIGHTING CHAPLAIN.

CHAPLAIN JOHN HOGARTH LOZIER.

Chaplain Lozier, 'the orator of the day, who made such a ringing, loyal speech on Memorial Day, was born in Indiana in 1830, and graduated from DePauw University in 1857. He served three years and three months as Chaplain of the 37th Regiment, Indiana Infantry, and two years as Major of the "Indiana Legion." The later years of his service were devoted to providing for the helpless soldiers, and their widows and orphans, prior to the founding of the Indiana Soldiers' Home, of which he was financial agent.

Among the many things written of him during the war, the following, copied from "The Annals of the Army of the Cumberland," pages 325 and 326, will be regarded as of special weight, from the fact that this book was compiled under the eye of Gen. Rosecrans, and was practically edited by the martyr President Garfield:

"As an instance of the valuable services rendered by the army chaplains, we may mention that during the battles of Stone River, Chaplain Lozier of the 37th Indiana was constantly on the ground assisting in the removal of the wounded, exposing himself in the most fearless manner to the shower of shot and shell. His services upon that occasion were of inestimable value, as can be attested by many who, but for him helpless and wounded as they were, might have met their death at the feet of the trampling hosts rushing on to the fray."

He was the first prohibition candidate for Governor of the State of Iowa, and was the founder of the Clear Lake Park, and Religous Summer Resort enterprise. He has the honor of being the first mover in the Iowa Tempeance Alliance, and drew the first draft of its articles of alliance. He was chosen its first president, but declined to serve because he was carrying the Clear Lake enterprise. He is now department chaplain of the Iowa G. A. R., and is extensively known among the boys in blue, not only in the State but the Nation. His home is at Mt. Vernon, where he has located, in order to afford his sons the advantages of Cornell College.

THE CHAPLAIN'S RHYMES

OF "TENDERFOOT" AND "GRAYBACK" TIMES.

[As recited by the author at the great National Camp Fire of the G. A. R. at San Francisco, August 1886, at the conclusion of the speeches of Comrades John A. Logan, O. O. Howard and Commander-in-Chief Lucius Fairchild].

I

Again on the "homeward march" are met
    The Veteran "Boys in Blue";
The boys who answered their country's call
    In sixty-one and two.
Boys who were boys in those lithsome days,
    That drift to the "Long Ago,"
And are still "the boys" in feats and joys,
    That only Veterans know.

"SHAKE."

II.

For when comrades meet, they whiles repeat,
    Their soldiering days of yore;
And renew the scenes (and the "Army Beans"),
    And fight their battles o'er.
And though they gaze, through a lengthening maze,
    Of years of toil and pain,
You marvel not, that,—those years forgot,—
    The "boys" are boys again.

III.

And the fife and drum make the young blood come
  In the Veteran's veins anew,
And he answers all the bugle calls,
  As in 'sixty-one and 'two
At Revilee he "scratches out,"
  With his old-time yawn and rub.
And, anon, you see him "scratching dirt"
  When he hears the call for "grub."

"And the fife and drum make the young blood come."

IV.

And the din and clatter of cup and platter,
  Brings old-time memories back,
When we first marched up with plate and cup
  To Uncle Samuel's "rack."
How our teeth did crack on the old "hard tack,"
  But failed to leave their "mark";
How we'd chew and gag over beef from some stag
  That descended from Noah's Ark!

"Uncle Samuel's 'Rack'."

V.

We had read in the Book that when devils forsook
    The victim they long had bound,
Into swine they fled, and, 'tis further said
    These swine—not the devils—were drowned.
Well, the "boys" relate, that the pork we ate,
    Along with our army beans,
Had come from some shoat that went afloat
    On that sea ot the Gadarenes!

VI.

And didn't we think it "mighty tough"
    When we *first* went into camp?
No boards were sent to floor our tent!
    And the evening dews were damp!
And you and I heaved many a sigh,
    And ruefully scratched our heads,
When we understood our "Uncle" would
    Not issue us *feather* beds!

"When we first went into camp."

VII.

And weren't those knapsacks hard as rocks,
    We woefully took for pillows?
And didn't those straw bunks torture us,
    With their undulating billows?
And didn't those letters *first* sent home,
    Their tidings of *hardships* utter?
We had to drink coffee without any *cream,*
    And sometimes were out of butter!"

VIII.

And 'tis funny now to remember how
    Our "tactics" we displayed,
As we tramped and trod in the "Awkward Squad"
    Of that "Tenderfoot Brigade."
With that everlasting "Left," "Left," "Left,"
    That drill with saber and gun;
And that "Double Quick"—well, it came too thick
    To be rated as first-class *fun.*

"In the 'Awkward Squad'."

IX.

But didn't we strut with princely pride
    When our uniforms we drew?
Coats big enough to take us inside,
    And our stolen poultry, too.
Pants—you say—"cut with a dull wood-saw,
    And made to fit the Buck,"
And you say yourselves that "Number Twelves"
    Were the smallest *shoes* you struck!

"And our stolen poultry, too."

X.

But though you "struck" no smaller shoes,
  The "*converse*" may be true:
If you happened to fool 'round a Government mule,
  Some smaller shoes struck *you!*
And whether or not you escaped his feet,
  I'm very certain that you'll
Admit the fact, that your throat you've cracked,
  By yelling "Here's Your Mule"

"Here's your mule!"

XI.

But the funny thing in our soldiering,
  Is how we thought it "tough."
When we first went in, with our tender skin,
  Though of *rations* we had enough.
But after we'd "been there" a year or two,
  The flat side of a rail
Was a "downy" bed; and "nigger bread"
  Was better than toast and quail!

XII.

For our stomachs grew much tougher, too,
  As well as our heels and hide;
And we didn't "gag" when a strolling mag—
  —Got in our meat we 'spied!
If he set up a "*Pre-emption Claim*"
  We didn't dispute his terms;
He held his claim; but, all the same,
  We went for that "Diet of Worms!"

"'That Diet of Worms!'"

XIII.

And our drinks from bogs where wallowed hogs
  Was like nectar that angels quaff!
And we gladly went for that old "Pup Tent;"
  —'Twas a palace when we got half.
And when we got where the fight was hot,
  Most any shelter would suit;
And when shot and shell around us fell,
  You're right we could "grab a root!"

      *   *   *   *   *   *

But we found short rations and scanty fare
  Before the disturbance was through,
But the "boys" declare that the *underwear*
  Was the *shortest* of all they drew.
You drew that shirt down over your head, —
  —Those drawers up over your feet;
But—short is the tale—you did always fail
  To cause those "extremes to meet!"

"The *shortest* of all we drew."

XV.

Or, to use the phrase of our soldiering days:
    That *underwear* "neglected
To close up the ranks and keep the flanks
    And center well protected!"
But "compensations" are everywhere,
    And e'en here we got our pay back—
As through that breach we chanced to reach
    And capture a straggling "Grayback."

XVI.

Ah! Comrades, what wonder you seem appalled?
    What queer sensations creep o'er us
At thought of that insect, technically called,
    "*Pediculous Corporis!*"
Now, if my meaning you fail to see
    In this ancient Roman name,
Just call it a *Blouse* and skip the ":B,"
    And youv'e caught it just the same!

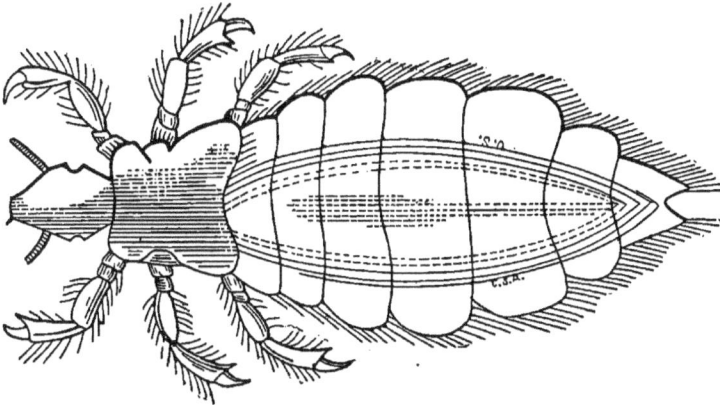

"Pediculus Corporis.

XVII.

Yet no soldier here will drop e'en a tear
    For his "gray" old "companions" of yore;
Tho' admitting the fact that they "stuck to your back"
    Through all the grim fortunes of war!

Thus prejudice patriotism o'erpowers;
  For no one among us denies
There was more "soldier blood" in their veins than in
        ours,
    In proportion, of course, to their *size!*

XVIII.

And who were more watchful and active than they,
  Amid all war's dreadful alarms?
You never attacked them by night or by day,
  But you found them "in force, under *arms!*"
You never betrayed them by guile or surprise,
  And nothing their ardor could smother;
If you caused them to "git" from a certain "arm'd pit,"
  You soon found them safe in the other!

"In force, under arms."

XIX.

And none of this "sectional hostility,"
  His generous nature e'er knew;
The friend of the traitorous rebel was he,
  As of Loyalty's legions in Blue.
When he and his family came to our camp,
  Full many a big tree and thicket,
Hid even you chaps who wore feathers and straps,
  While you did "private" duty on *pick it!*

"Private duty on *pick it.*"

XX.

Of course your big officers would not confess
    To these "naked facts" when you'd "tree" 'em,
But would boldly declare they had only been there
    . To drill for the army *lice-see-'em!*—(Lyceum).
If "practice makes perfect" we all will admit,
    That going so often to "train" ment,
That, "stripped for the strife," they would *sacrifice life,*
    To make that a "crack" entertainment.

*XXI.

And now, unlamented by "Reb" or by "Yank,"
    The Grayback in solitude sleepeth;
But the chases we gave him o'er breastwork and flank,
    Each Veteran's fond memory keepeth;
In "foraging off" of the country" he beat
    "Old Billy" the marcher and "bummer";
And none of us doubt that he *did* "fight it out"
    Like Grant, though it *took him all summer!*
      *   *   *   *   *

XXII.

It is probably best that I "give you a rest,"
  Though it be not the "rest" of my rhyme.
With so "lively" a theme, it would naturally seem
  That you don't want *too much* at a time.
I'm glad if my rhymes of our soldiering· times
  Shall add to your measure of joys;
For my *subject* I know, in those days long ago,
  Has "tickled" the most of you "Boys!"

"PARADE'S DISMISSED."

IS OUR BANNER STILL ADVANCING?*

BY CHAPLAIN LOZIER.

[NOTE—All who witnessed the charge of the Union troops upon Missionary Ridge will remember that the whole face of the mountain soon became enveloped in smoke and dust, so that it was at times difficult to distinguish our lines of Union Soldiers save by the bright colors of the glorious old "Stars and Stripes." Hence, all eyes were strained to catch a glimpse of our Banner, and all were inquiring: "Is she still going up?" Then again the "Old Flag" would be seen through the rifts in the smoke and dust, still mounting toward the top, and then there would go up a shout that made Lookout Mountain and the Forts around Chattanooga re-echo:—"Yes, she's still going higher and higher! These incidents gave rise to the following songs or recitations].

"Is our Banner still advancing?"
  Hear the loyal hosts exclaim,
While the rallying ranks of freedom,
  Onward dash 'mid smoke and flame,
Onward up the fort ribbed mountain
  'Gainst the leaden storm they passed,
Till the grand old Flag of Freedom,
  Waved in triumph o'er its crest!

All songs marked* are published in sheet music, and can be had by mail, by sending 30 cents to the S. Bainards' Sons, or Root & Son's Music Co., Chicago, or the John Church Music Co., Cincinnati, O.

"Is our Banner still advancing?"
  Gasped the soldier as he died,
While the blood his heart was yielding,
  Trickled down the mountain side.
But his comrades hurried onward,
  Till the mountain top they trod!
They have scaled that dreaded mountain,
  He has scaled the "mount of God!"

"Is our Banner still advancing?"
  Rings the echo through the air;
Well may freemen swell that chorus,
  All their hopes are centered there.
Bear aloft that grand old Banner
  While our rallying hosts repeat:
"This shall be our nation's glory,
  Or our nation's winding sheet!"

CHORUS:—Still advancing, Higher! Higher!
      Shout ye loyal! Shout ye brave!
      Tyrants, let your hopes expire,
      When you see that Banner wave!

YES, OUR FLAG IS STILL ADVANCING.*

Reply to the preceding.—Same author.

Yes! Our Flag is still advancing!
  See! It mounts toward the sun!
Rebel legions dash against it,
  But it still keeps moving on!
  *See page 14.

Traitors aim their deadly missiles,
　　Monarchs frown across the main,
But the foe of human freedom
　　Aims and frowns and strikes in vain!

Yes!　Our Flag is still advancing!
　　As yon radiant orb of day,
Mounting to its heavenly zenith,
　　Makes the shadows fade away.
So our Flag dispels oppression;
　　Lo!　'Tis Freedom's rising sun!
Earth's last fetter shall be broken,
　　E'er its radiant race is run.

Yes!　Our Flag is still advancing!
　　How these words our bosoms thrill!
May our sons in coming ages,
　　Keep that Flag advancing still.
Till, o'er all this vast dominion,
　　Where the foot of man hath trod,
All shall bow 'neath Freedom's Banner,
　　All shall worship Freedom's God!

CHORUS:—Still advancing!　O!　We hail t ee!
　　　　In thy grandeur ever wave!
　　　　Perish all who dare assail thee,
　　　　Grand old Banner of the Brave!

THE OLD UNION WAGON.*

Written the day before we marched on " Stone River." During which
battle the *Emancipation Proclamation* went into effect.

BY JOHN HOGARTH LOZIER.

Air—" Wait for the Wagon."—Key of C.

1

In Uncle Sam's dominion, in eighteen sixty-one,
The fight between Secession and Union was begun;
The South declared they'd have the "rights" which Uncle Sam denied
Or in their Secesh Wagon they'd all take a ride.

CHORUS—Hurrah for the Wagon, the old Union Wagon!
We'll stick to our wagon and all take a ride.

2

The makers of our wagon were men of solid wit,
They made it out of "Charter Oak" that would not rot or *split*.
Its wheels are of material the strongest and the best,
And two are named the North and South, and two the East and West

3

Our wagon bed is strong enough for any "revolution,"
In fact, 'tis the "hull" of the "old Constitution;"
Her coupling's strong, her axle's long, and anywhere you get her,
No Monarch's frown can "back her down"—no Traitor can *upset* her.
*See page 14.

4

This good old Union Wagon. the nations all admired;
Her wheels had run for four score years and never once been "tired."
Her passengers were happy as long her way she whirled,
For the good old Union Wagon was the glory of the world!

5

But when old Abram took command, the South wheel got displeased
Because the "public fat" was gone that kept her axle *greased;*
And when he gathered up the reins and started on his route,
She plunged into secession and knocked some "fellers" out!

6

Now while in this secession mire the wheel was sticking tightly,
Some Tory passengers got mad and swore at Abra'm slightly;
But Abra'm "couldn't see it," so he didn't heed their clatter—
"There's *"too much black mud on the wheel,"* says he, "that's what's the
    matter."

7

So Abra'm gave them notice that in eighteen sixty-three,
Unless the rebels "dried it up," h'ed make their slaves all free;
And then the man that led the van to fight against his nation,
Would drop his gun and home he'd run, to fight against starvation.

8

When Abra'm said he'd free the slaves that furnished their supplies,
It opened Northern traitors' *mouths* and Southern traitors' *eyes.*
"The slaves." said they, "will *run away* if you thus rashly free them!"
But Abra'm 'guessed, perhaps, they'd best go home and *oversee* them!"

9

Around our Union Wagon our loyal hosts stood fast,
And brought her through the struggle all safe and sound at last!
And of all the Generals high or low, that helped to save the nation,
There's none that struck a harder blow than General *Emancipation!*

WHEN SHERMAN MARCHED DOWN TO THE SEA.

By CHAPLAIN LOZIER.

Air—" Red, White and Blue."

All hail to the heroes of Sherman!
   The " Bonnie Blue Boys" of the West,
The pride and the boast of the Nation,
   The truest and bravest and best.
Twas these who in triumph bore o'er them,
   That gallant old flag of the free,
And drove all opposers before them,
   When Sherman marched down to the Sea.

They came from the bench and the anvil,
   The forest, the field and the shop;
And when they took aim at a Rebel,
   Then something was certain to *drop*.
And theirs was the nerve that could lead them
   Wherever their chief might decree;
And naught could withstand or impede them,
   When Sherman marched down to the Sea.

All hail to the heroes of freedom
   Who fought 'neath the Stripes and the Stars,
Ye all are the greatest of victors,
   Who won in the greatest of wars.
But none has a future before him,
   More freighted with honors than he,
Who fought with our flag floating o'er him,
   When Sherman marched down to the Sea.

HAIL TO THE LEGIONS OF THE WEST.*

By CHAPLAIN LOZIER.

Hail to the Legions of the West!
A hundred crimson fields of glory,
For them proclaim that fadeless fame
That breathes in song and lives in story.
With iron will and dauntless breast,
They *strike* to save the land that bore them.
Hail to the Legions of the West,
Who bear that grand old banner o'er them!

Hands that have felled the forest oak
And torn the towering cliffs assunder;
Hands that the virgin soil have broke,
And made the sledge and anvil thunder;
These are the hands by Heaven blest,
That drove our vanquished foes before them.
Hail to the Legions of the West,
Who bear our grand old banner o'er them!

Since Sumpter's stars and stripes went down,
How dark the Nation's night of sorrow;
But, thanks to God, the night is gone,
And brighter, purer dawns the morrow.
Back to the South,—no more oppressed,—
They bare our banners to restore them.
Hail to the Legions of the West,
Who bear our grand old banner o'er them!

*See page 13.

OUR PROTEST AGAINST TOADYISM TO TRAITORS.

By MAJOR J. H. LOZIER.

Go stand within those *prison pens*,
   Where our starved martyr's dust is lying.
Brave men, to whom the battle field
   Had been a luxury in dying.
Go ask those wasted spectral forms,
   Whence dread starvation drove their spirits;
Tho' voiceless, they with thundering tones,
   Will tell the fate that that treason merits.

Go stand beside the *nameless graves*,
   Strewn o'er a hundred fields of glory.
Speak to the heroes sleeping there
   Coffined in garments stiff and gory.
And, though their tongue give back no sound,
   To plead for vengeance on this treason,
Their blood, still "crying from the ground,"
   Speaks louder in the ear of reason.

Go ask the *widow* o'er whose path
   Hang shadows of untold sorrow;
What pinching poverty she hath!
   How dark her bodings of the morrow!
Ask her, and fifty thousand more
   Whose widow tears Jehovah measures,
Whose fondest hopes are crimsoned o'er,
   And buried with their perished treasures.

Go ask the *orphan*, for whose weal
   A father's dying prayer was spoken,
Mid callous hearts—too proud to feel,
   A wanderer, homeless and heartbroken.
A youth without the fond caress
   That gilds the after years with gladness;
An orphan's heart, whose loneliness
   Is eloquent with silent sadness.

Go ask that *parent*, bending low,
　That stricken sire, that mourning mother;
Theirs is a bitterness of woe,
　Known to their hearts, their God, no other.
They gave their boy, they only know
　That somewhere his dead form is sleeping.
Ask them what justice claims, and lo!
　You hear the answer in their weeping!

Go ask that *maimed* and shattered brave,
　Thy spirit bowing low before him;
Part of his body fills the grave,
　He gave *that* for the land that bore him,
In every scar there seems a tongue,
　Whose plaintive pleadings none can number;
Crying, "How long, O Lord! how long
　Shall justice blush and vengeance slumber?"

Go ask that half a million men
　Who drove that traitorous horde before them;
Who stormed their citidels, and then
　Planted their grand old banner o'er them!
Ask them, and heed their answer well,
　" *Give treason less of exaltation!*"
Or whispered mutterings may swell
　To *thunders* that shall shake the nation.

Trust not this government to hands,
　That yesterday had gladly slain thee!
But trust it to those loyal bands,
　Whose lives were periled to sustain thee!
Care for those *stricken ones*, who weep,
　Not for the *fiends* who caused their weeping!
Honor the graves where *patriots* sleep,
　Who but for treason were not sleeping!

THE NAMELESS GRAVES WHERE OUR COMRADES LIE.*

By CHAPLAIN LOZIER.

Hark! Hear ye not that plaintive tone,
That comes like the ocean's dying moan?
'Tis the ling'ring strain which the angels play,
O'er the graves where the nation's heroes lay.

Comrades we loved in life's fresh bloom,
Have been laid to rest in the warrior's tomb,
The silver cord has been rent in twain,
And the angels have gathered them "Home Again."

Sad are our hearts, for their lights are fled,
And their treasures sleep with the nation's dead;
But Faith stoops low on its radiant wing,
And bids us Hark! while the angels sing!

From the field of strife where the patriot dies,
There's a shining pathway that mounts the skies;
And the tongue that shouts our hosts along,
May swell the note of the angels' song.

Let us love them still, for although we part,
There's a ray of hope for the saddest heart;
'Tis the hope that when life's last march is o'er,
We shall camp where comrades part no more.

Chorus—Sweet be their rest, calm their repose,
      Safe from the reach of mortal woes;
      For we know that death is a transient pain,
      If beyond the River we meet again.

*See page 14.

WE'LL FIGHT IT OUT HERE ON THE OLD UNION LINE.*

[Written by Chaplain Lozier for the National Republican Convention that first nominated General Grant for President, and sung by him from the platform, immediately after the General was nominated, assisted by George F. Root, Chaplain C. C. McCabe and Major Frank Lumbard].

We'll rally again to the standard we bore
Over battle-fields crimson and gory;
Shouting, "Hail to the Chief who in Freedom's fierce war,
Hath covered that Banner with glory!"

CHORUS—Then rally again! Then rally again!
With the soldier and sailor and "*bummer;*"
And we'll fight it out here on the old Union line,
No odds if "it takes us all summer!"

We'll rally again by the side of the men
Who breasted the conflict's fierce rattle;
And they'll find us still true who were true to them then,
And bade them "God speed" in the battle.

We'll rally again! and that Flag of the Free.
Shall *stay* where our heroes have placed it,
And ne'er shall they govern on land or on sea
Whose treason hath spurned and disgraced it.

We'll rally again and our motto shall be,—
—Whatever the nation that bore us;—
God bless that old Banner, the Flag of the Free,
And all who would live with it o'er us!

*See page 13.

BLUE COAT AND MISS DIXIE.

A rhymed interview. such as you and I have had with Secesh Women. Introducing some of their peculiar words and ways.

By the "FIGHTING CHAPLAIN."

1—A jolly young Blue Coat was walking his "beat,"
When lo! a fair damsel came sailing down street.
The sight was so rare to the soldier boy's eye
That he came to a "front" till the lady passed by.

2—The Star Spangled Banner hung out o'er the street,
And as she glanced upward she happened to see't,
Then stopped, her "Secesh" maledictions to utter,
And just to get 'round it, *walked out in the gutter*.

3—Said she, "how I hate that detestable rag!
I swan, hit can't whip our Confederit flag;
We'll soon drive you *Lincoln Dogs* off from our doors,
And then *take your banners to mop up our floors*."

4—So struck was the "Yank" with her dazzling charms
He felt half inclined to present her his arms,
When lo! she approached him with elegant grace
And gently attempted to *spit in his face!*

5—It happened just then that he bowed very low,
A mark of respect to the lady, you know;
And so the mild missile her sweet lips had sped,
As good luck would have it, went over his head!

6—Said he, "gentle maiden, thy form so divine,
Reminds me so much of a sweetheart of mine;
She lives far away in the Land of the Free,
And she likes all the 'Blue Coats,' and specially *me*."

7—Said she, "Northern women is hideous jades!
A passel of ignorant *strappin milkmaids*,
While *weuns* is *culchered* and *larnt*, and refined, too,
And we *toat* all the money that *weuns is mind to*."

8—We Southerners is the superior race,
And only was teaching you Yankees your place;
When *you alls* got mad and our country infested,
While *we alls never had none of you alls milested*."

9—"Fair lady, you say that our women are fools,
And yet they have always been teaching your schools!
If fools make best teachers, it strikes me as queer
That you should send North when you've so many here."

10—"You impudent Yankee! You mudsill! You brute ye!
If I had a pistol, I'd take *hit* and shoot ye!
You've *pestered* me now till I'm likin' to faint,
But that would please *you ens* too well, so I *shaint!*"

11—"Fair damsel, I'm going! Here comes the Relief,
But these are my views of your 'ladies' in brief:
Your 'colors' are false, like piratical skippers!
In looks you're all 'Ducks,' but in snuff you're all 'Dippers.'"

BARBARA FRIETCHIE.—JOHN G. WHITTIER.

Up from the meadows rich with corn,
Clear in the cool September morn,

The clustered spires of Frederick stand,
Green-walled by the hills of Maryland.

Round about them orchards sweep,
Apple and peach tree fruited deep,

Fair as a garden of the Lord,
To the eyes of the famished rebel horde,

On that pleasant morn of the early Fall,
When Lee marched over the mountain wall,

Over the mountains winding down,
Horse and foot, into Frederick town.

Forty flags with their silver stars,
Forty flags with their crimson bars,

Flapped in the morning wind: the sun
Of noon looked down, and saw not one.

Up rose old Barbara Frietchie then,
Bowed with her four score years and ten;

Bravest of all in Frederick town,
She took up the flag the men hauled down.

In her attic-window the staff she set,
To show that one heart was loyal yet.

Up the street came the rebel tread,
Stonewall Jackson riding ahead.

Under his slouched hat left and right
He glanced: the old flag met his sight.

"Halt!"—the dust-brown ranks stood fast;
"Fire!"—out blazed the rifle-blast.

It shivered the window, pane and sash,
It rent the banner with seam and gash.

Quick, as it fell from the broken staff,
Dame Barbara snatched the silken scarf;

She leaned far out on the the window-sill,
And shook it forth with a royal will.

"Shoot, if you must, this old gray head,
But spare your country's flag," she said.

A shade of sadness, a blush of shame,
Over the face of the leader came;

The nobler nature within him stirred
To life at that woman's deed and word.

"Who touches a hair of yon gray head
Dies like a dog! March on!" he said.

All day long through Frederick street
Sounded the tread of marching feet;

All day long that free flag tossed
Over the heads of the rebel host.

Ever its torn folds rose and fell
On the loyal winds that loved it well;

And through the hill-gaps sunset light
Shone over it with a warm good-night.

Barbara Frietchie's work is o'er,
And the rebel rides on his raids no more.

Honor to her! and let a tear
Fall, for her sake, on Stonewall's bier.

Over Barbara Frietchie's grave,
Flag of Freedom and Union, wave!

Peace and order and beauty draw
Round thy symbol of light and law;

And ever the stars above look down
On thy stars below in Frederick town.

THE DUTCH BARBARA FRITCHIE.

Id vas droo der streeds of Fridricksdown,
Der red hot zun he vas shine him down.

Bast der zaloons all filt mit beer,
Der rebel vellers walkt on deir ear.

All day droo Fridricksdown zo fast,
Horses, und guns, und zogers bast.

Der rebel flag! he shone him oud so bridt
As if, by Jinks, he got some ridt!

Vere vas dat Onion Flag? Der zun
He shone him down not on a von!

Up jumped dot olt Miss Fritchie den,
Zo olt by nine score years und ten.

She grabbed up der flag der rebels haul down
Und fasen it quick py dot nidt-gown.

Den she sat py der vinder, ver all could see,
Der vas *von* vat lofe dot flag so free!

Pertty soon cum riden up Stonewall Jack,
Sitten py der middle of his horse's back.

Under him brow he squint him eyes:
Dot Flag! Dot make him great surprise!

"Halt!" Every veller make him sdill;
"Fire!" Vas echoed from hill to hill.

I'd bursted der strings from dot nidt-gown,
But Barbara Fritchie she was arount!

She grabbed up der flag again so quick
Und oud of her vinder her arms did sdick

"Obuse ef you would dis olt balt head,
But leave alone dot flag," she said.

Zo soon zo quick as Jack could do
He holler him out mit his face so blue:

"Halt! Don'd you fire anunder gun!
You quits, py jeminy, efery von!"

"Who bull a hair oud of dot balt head,
Dies awful quick! Go aheat!" he said.

Und all dot day, und all dot nidt,
Till efery rebel vas oud of sight,

Und leaf behindt him dot Fridricksdown,
Dot flag! He vas stickin py dot nidt-gown!

Dame Barbara Fritchie's vork is done,
She vas vone vooman as don'd would run!

Bully for her! Und drop a tear
For dot olt vooman mitoud some fear.

I vould drink her heldt mit zwi glass beer,
If I don'd vas afraid I can't got some here.

"Come here, you inquisitive rascal."

THE FRONTIER VETERAN TO HIS GRANDSON.

[As recited by Judge F. P. Cochrane, of Cottonwood Falls, Kansas, late Lieutenant on Generals Negley and Tom Woods' Staffs, Army of the Cumberland, to whom the publisher is indebted for the poem].

BY CAPT. JACK CRAWFORD.

I.

Hold on! hold on! My goodness, you take my breath, my son,
A firin' questions at me like shot from a Gatlin' gun.
Why do I wear this eagle, an' flag, an' brazen star?
An' why do my old eyes glisten when somebody mentions war?
An' why do I call men comrades? and why do my eyes grow bright,
When you hear me tell your grandma, "I'm going to Post to-night?"
Come here, you inquisitive rascal! and sit on your grandpa's knee,
An' I'll try an' answer the broadsides you've been firin' at me.

II.

Away back in the sixties, an' long before you were born,
The news came flashin' to us one bright an' sunny morn,
That some of our southern neighbors, a thinkin', no doubt, 'twas right,
Had trained their guns on our banner, an' opened a nasty fight.
The great big guns war' a boomin', an' the shot flyin' thick an' fast,
An' troops all over the southland war' rapidly bein' massed,
When a *thrill* went through the Nation, a fear that our glorious land
Might be split an' divided an' ruined by a Southern traitor band.

III.

Whew! but warn't there excitement, an' didn't the boys' eyes flash,
An' didn't we curse them rebels fur bein' so foolish an' rash?
And didn't we raise the neighbors with loud an' continued cheers,
When Old Abe sent out a docyment a callin' fór volunteers! ,
An' didn't we rush to the school house, where the people was axt to
    meet?
An' didn't we flock to the colors, when the drums began to beat?
An' didn't the people cheer us when we got aboard the cars,
With the flag a wavin' o'er us, an' went away to the wars?

IV.

I'll never forgit your grandma, as she stood outside o' the train,
Her face as white as a snowdrift, her tears a fallin' like rain—
She stood there quiet an' deathlike, amid all the rush an' noise—
Fur the war was a takin' from her, her husband and three brave boys,
Bill, Charley an' little Tommy—just turned eighteen, but as true
An' gallant a little soldier as ever wore the blue—
It seemed almost like murder for to tear her poor heart so,
But your grandpa *couldn't* stay, baby, and the boys war' determined
    to go.

V.

The evenin' afore we started, she called the boys to her side,
An' told 'em as how they war' alwrys their mother' joy an' pride,
An' though her soul was in torture, an' her poor heart bleedin' an'
    sore,   .
An' though she needed her darlin's, their country needed them more,
An' she told them to be as lovin' and kind as they were at home,
An' told 'em to do their duty, where'er their feet might roam,
An' if (an' the tears nigh choked her) they fell in front o' the foe,
She'd go to her blessed Saviour an' ax Him to lighten the blow.

VI.

Bill lays an' awaits the summons 'neath Spottsyvania's sod,
An' on the field of Antietam Charlie's spirit went back to God,
An' Tommy, our baby Tommy, we buried one starlight night,
Along with his fallen comrades, just after the Wilderness fight—
The lightnin' struck our family tree, an' stripped it of every limb,
A leavin' only this bare old trunk a standin' alone an' grim!
My boy, that's why your grandma, when you kneel to the God you
    love,
Makes you ax Him to watch your uncles, an' make 'em happy above.

VII.

That's why you sometimes see her with tear drops in her eyes—
That's why you sometimes catch her a tryin' to hide her sighs—
That's why at our great reunions she looks so solemn an' sad—
That's why her heart seems a breakin' when the boys seem jolly an'
     glad;
That's why you sometimes find her in the bedroom overhead,
Down on her knees a prayin', with their pictures on the bed ;
That's why the old-time brightness will light up her face no more
Till she meets her hero warriors in the camp on the other shore.

VIII.

Well! when the great war was over, back came the veterans true,
With not one star amissin' from that azure field of blue ;
An' the boys, who in the battle had stood the fiery test,
Formed Posts of the great Grand Army in the north, south, east and
     west.
Fraternity, Charity, Loyalty, is the motto 'neath which they train—
Their object to care for the helpless, an' banish sorrow an' pain
From the homes o' the widows an' orphans o' the boys who have gone
     before
To answer their names at roll call, in that Great Grand Army Corps.

IX.

An' that's why we wear these badges,—the eagle an' flag an' star,
Worn only by veteran heroes who fought in that bloody war.
An' that's why my ol' eyes glisten when talkin' about the fray,
An' that's why these gray old veterans keep clingin' together to-day,
An' that's why I tell your grandma, "I'm goin' to Post to-night;"
For there's where I meet the ol' boys who stood with me in the fight,
An', my child, that's why I've taught you to love an' revere the men
Who come here a wearin' badges, to fight those battles again.

X.

For they are the gallant heroes, who stood 'mid the shot an' shell,
An' follered the flyin' colors right into the mouth of—well!
They are the men whose valor saved the land from disgrace an shame
An' lifted her back in triumph to her perch on the dome of fame ;
An' as long as you live, my darlin', till your lips in death are mute,
When you see that badge on a bosom, take off your hat an' salute ;
An' if any ol' vet should halt you, an' question you why you do,
Just tell him you've got a *right* to, for your granddad's a comrade too!

GLORY! GLORY! HALLELUJAH!

John Brown's body lies a mould'ring in the grave,
John Brown's body lies a mould'ring in the grave,
John Brown's body lies a mould'ring in the grave.
    His soul is marching on.

    CHORUS.—Glory, glory, hallelujah;
          Glory, glory, hallelujah;
          Glory, glory, hallelujah;
            His soul is marching on.

The stars of heaven are looking kindly down,
The stars of heaven are looking kindly down,
The stars of heaven are looking kindly down,
    On the grave of old John Brown.—CHORUS.

He's gone to be a soldier in the army of the Lord,
He's gone to be a soldier in the army of the Lord,
He's gone to be a soldier in the army of the Lord,
    His soul is marching on.—CHORUS.

John Brown's knapsack is strapped upon his back,
John Brown's knapsack is strapped upon his back,
John Brown's knapsack is strapped upon his back,
    His soul is marching on.—CHORUS.

His pet lambs will meet him on the way,
His pet lambs will meet him on the way,
His pet lambs will meet him on the way,
    And they'll go marching on.—CHORUS.

We'll hang Jeff Davis to a sour apple tree,
We'll hang Jeff Davis to a sour apple tree,
Old Andy didn't do it, but still it ought to be,
    As we go marching on.—CHORUS.

SHERIDAN'S RIDE,—THOMAS BUCHANAN READ.

Up from the South at break of day,
Bringing to Winchester fresh dismay,
The affrighted air with a shudder bore,
Like a herald in haste, to the chieftain's door,
The terrible grumble, and rumble, and roar,
Telling the battle was on once more,
And Sheridan twenty miles away.

And wider still those billows of war
Thundered along the horizon's bar;
And louder yet into Winchester rolled
The roar of that red sea uncontrolled,
Making the blood of the listener cold,
As he thought of the stake in that fiery fray,
And Sheridan twenty miles away.

But there is a road from Winchester town,
A good, broad highway leading down;
And there through the flush of the morning light,
A steed as black as the steeds of night,
Was seen to pass, as with eagle flight.
As if he knew the terrible need,
He stretched away with his utmost speed;
Hills rose and fell; but his heart was gay,
With Sheridan fifteen miles away.

Still sprung from those swift hoofs, thundering South,
The dust, like smoke from the cannon's mouth;
Or the trail of a comet, sweeping faster and faster,
Foreboding to traitors the doom of disaster.
The heart of the steed and the heart of the master
Were beating like prisoners assaulting their walls,
Impatient to be where the battle-field calls;
Every nerve of the charger was strained to full play,
With Sheridan only ten miles away.

Under his spurning feet, the road
Like an arrowy Alpine river flowed,
And the landscape sped away behind
Like an ocean flying before the wind,
And the steed, like bark fed with furnace ire,
Swept on, with his wild eye full of fire.
But lo! he is nearing his heart's desire;
He is snuffing the smoke of the roaring fray,
With Sheridan only five miles away.

The first that the General saw were the groups
Of stragglers, and then the retreating troops;
What was done,—what to do,—a glance told him both,
And striking his spurs, with a terrible oath,
He dashed down the line, 'mid a storm of huzzas,
And the wave of retreat checked its course there, because
The sight of the master compelled it to pause.
With foam and with dust the black charger was gray;
By the flash of his eye, and his red nostril's play,
He seemed to the whole great army to say,
"I have brought you Sheridan all the way,
From Winchester down, to save the day."

Hurrah, hurrah for Sheridan!
Hurrah, hurrah for horse and man!
And when their statues are placed on high,
Under the dome of the Union sky,—
The American soldiers' Temple of Fame,

There with the glorious General's name
Be it said in letters both bold and bright
" Here is the steed that saved the day
By carrying Sheridan into the fight,
From Winchester,—twenty miles away !"

SHAKE SHNYDER'S RIDE.

Dot vas een der repellion, away down sout
Und der pattle von Vinchester vos youst broke out,
'Tvas a leedle before daylighd, und dere on der grount,
Shkattered about here und dere, vas der troops shleeping sount
Und der roosders vas growing een der henkoops arount,
Ven all ov a suddenly somedings vas der matter.
Aboud tain tousand cannons all gommenced to klatter,
Und dot shkared all der boys, und dey gommenced to shkatter.

Shake Shnyder vas dere; he vas a raw regruit,
Und so gwick vhen he heard der cannon shoot
He dought it vas better vor heem to shkoot.
So an olt gray hoss stood near by een der vagon track,
Und Shake bicked ub a shtick und hees olt knap-sack,
Und een youst one shoomp he vas on hees back,
Und he shtruck dot old horse a vearful krack,
Und he yelled mit all hees might, "You git,"
Und avay he vent down der road lickerty shplit.

Py Jinks! right avay der olt hoss shtruck hees gait,
Mit his head und his tail both shticken out sdraight;
But dot vasnt all, now hold on, you youst vait!
'Tvas youst five o'clock ven he shdarted dot day,
Und in tain minutes by der vatch Shake vas five milse avay.

Der road vas ruff und covered mit shtone,
But der olt gray hoss kept right on goin.
Ov course, vonce een a vhile he would let out a groan,
Vor dots drue, he vas notting but skin und bone.
But avay he vent, mitout bridle or saddle,
Und venefer he heard der sound ov der battle,
He vould git up and git, und hees olt hoofs vould rattle,
Vile Shake hung to hees back und made heem shkedaddle,
Und at dwenty minutes past five, by der tick ov der vatch,
Shake was tain milse avay, by Shiminy Krotch!

Py Grashus! dot vos a vearful ride;
But still Shake didnt vas satisfied,
He vanted to git furder avay vrom dot fighd.
So avay he vent down der roat, flying pell-mell,
Und he hurryed up der hoss, vor he knowed very vell
Vrom der vay dot der rebels vas firing der shell,
Ov he didn't shkedaddle he'd git shot, sure as——vell,

You know how 'tvas yourseluf, een a case like dot,
Ven der rebels vas chasin you pooty blamed hot,
Und you had to run like a sonovagun, By——Scott!
Oxpectin aifry minute to git your back full of shot.
Vell, dot vas der case mit Shake; 'tvas hees only salwation;
So he made dot hoss go like——all creation.
Und at half-past five by der sun dot day,
Shake Shyder vas fifdeen milse avay.

Und shdill on dey vent, raisin der dust,
Und aifry time dot a shell vood busht
'Tvas hard to tell vitch vas shkared der vurst.
Und Shake vas afraid on anudder account,
For he veighed two hunnerd und forty pount,
Und der vay der olt hoss got over der grount,
He dought aifry minute 'twould come to pass
Dot der olt hoss vould shtop und let heem go to grass.
But he vas meesdaken; avay dey vent down der road,
As if der tyful vas afder dem boad.
Und at twenty minutes ov six, youst oxactly to a tick,
Shake vas dwenty milse avay—vasnt dot pooty gwick?

Py Shemeny! dot olt hoss vas a buster to travel,
Und dot morning Shake made der olt vellar shkratch gravel;
Und Shnyder kept time ven der hosses feet come up,
Und he'd say, keep-it-up, keep-it-up, keep-it-up.
Und likewise dat hoss had lots of backbone—
You could tell dot vas so by der vay Shake vould groan.
But he vas bound to hang on ov it shplit heem in two,
So he hung like dem "kraybacks"—vell, vot else could he do?
Till at last der olt hoss begun to look pale,
Und der sweat run in shtreams off der end of hees tail.

So Shake dought by dese time it must be six, ainyhow,
Und he says to himself, I vas safe enough now.
So he shtopped and turned round, and what do you shpose?
He give der rebels der pass-word from der end of hees nose!
Und den he laffed at der rebels, vot vas left in de rear,
Vor he vas more as *dwenty-five* miles avay from dere!

So den hurrah for Shake Snyder, und dree cheers vor dot hoss,
Vor dots no use dalkin, dot olt gray vas boss.

Talk bout Sheridan's nag—vy, between you und me,
Der olt gray vould beat heem five dimes out ov dree.

So den let us cheer heem dhree times good und lout;
Already, now, Hu——vy, vats der matter mit your mout?
Oh, you can aiferyvone laff: dots all very vell,
But of you vas een Shnyder's place, how you vould yell.

Vy, here's Mr. Schmidt on der platform to-night; .
He vas a goot soldier ov course, dots all right;
But he got schkart at a rebel een dot wery same fight,
Und he got up und shkedaddled mid all of hees might,
Und een less' in tain minutes he vas glear out of sight!

Vell, ven such men got schkart, you oxpect Shake to keep cool?
Ov you do, you must dink he's a blasted olt fool.

Ov course, Shake got schkart, und run avay from dot strife;
But he couldn't do ainy different to safe hees life.

Besides, it vas safer—und vell did he know,
A live Dutchman vas better den a dead hero.

NO FIGHTIN' IN HEAVEN, BOYS.

ORT HOWELL, OF PERRY, IOWA, IN THE GRAND ARMY ADVOCATE

" You soldiers was havin' a meetin' " they said,
　A Grand Army camp-fire, or somethin' or other;
And I thought as how I'd just come in the stead
　Of Jimmy—you knowed 'im ?　Well, boys, I'm his mother.

Your ranks are a thinnin' an' every roll-call,
　Death answers for some, the *missin'*, you know,—
They fight in the battle of life an' they fall,
　Worn out an' a bleedin', they give up an' go

My heart was a soljer—it answered the call
　With Jimmy,—got wounded with him, an' it fell
Beside him in battle—then went through all;
　His starvin' an' sufferin' at that *prison hell.*

He wrote lots of letters, a tellin' so cheerful
　Of comrades, an' camp, an' the fun that they had;
He spoke of the sunshine, but was very keerful
　To leave out the shadder, an' things that was sad.

He said you had plenty to eat an' to wear,—
　Had two kinds of coffee, the ' plain black ' an' ' riled,'
An' two kinds of meat on the bill of fare,
　One's ' hog meat ' an' t'other is ' hog meat *spiled.*'

He writ me that sometimes your *colors* got mixed,
　He must have been jokin', (he had a great knack
Of talkin' in fun,) but he said coats was fixed
　.With blue all in front, but they all had gray-backs.

He said there was millions in one grand division
　All under command of—General Hardtack;
And detailed to work on old army provision,
　Such as stood rather long in the old haversack.

He said how at Petersburg blue coats and gray,
  Would visit an' trade when the fightin' would slack,
You swapped them coffee for tobacker, and they
  Swapped you their fresh corncake for wormy hardtack.

Do you know what it is boys to wait an' to wait,
  With hope an' dispair both a shakin' your soul?
I waited two years, boys, to find out his fate
  After seein' his name on the prisoners roll.

Oh, the torturin' pain of that waitin, an' waitin',
  Of hopin', disparin'; disparin' an' hopin'—
The gates of my heaven kept creakin' an' gratin'
  With openin' an' closin', an' closin' an' openin'.

An' wnen he came home, boys, my old heart was sadder
  To see him again, than when it was smote
With his partin' good-by. Oh, God! what a shadder!
  Just his bones, an' his soul, and an' old army coat!

Tears would not stay back, boys; I couldn't help cryin';
  I thought of the times that I'd rocked 'im to sleep
In my arms—a wee babe—a man now, an' dyin'—
  Yes, dyin' by inches, boys; wouldn't *you* weep?

He was patient an' cheerful, an' still kept a tryin'
  To hide his condition, (my old eyes was dim),
He told funny stories, was careful of sighin',
  But I heard Death whisperin', "*Jim, Come, Jim.*"

When God brought the springtime an' flowers of May,
  An' the sunshine peeped into each half open rose,
He said, 'Good bye, Mother,' an' went far away,
  Leavin me, an' a grave, an' his dear soljer close.

Who'll answer that record the death angels took
  Of slaughter with saber, with shot, an' with shell?
Who'll answer for blood-stains on God's record book?
  An' the sorrow in heaven, an' laughin' in hell?

When Judgment day brings us the last Grand Review,
  Who'll answer to God for this horrible crime?
No fightin' in heaven, that's one thing that's true!
  And I know I'll find Jim in that glorious clime.

SONG OF A THOUSAND YEARS.

BY HENRY C. WORK.

Lift up your eyes, desponding freemen!
　Fling to the winds your needless fears!
He who unfurl'd your beauteous banner,
　Says it shall wave a thousand years!

CHORUS.

　"A thousand years!" my own Columbia!
　　'Tis the glad day so long foretold!
　'Tis the glad morn whose early twilight
　　Washington saw in times of old.

What if the clouds, one little moment,
　Hide the blue sky where morn appears—
When the bright sun, that tints them crimson,
　Rises to shine a thousand years!—CHORUS.

Tell the great world these blessed tidings!
　Yes, and be sure the bondman hears;
Tell the oppress'd of ev'ry nation,
　Jubilee lasts a thousand years!—CHORUS.

Envious foes, beyond the ocean!
　Little we heed your threat'ning sneers;
Little will they—our children's children—
　When you are gone a thousand years.—CHORUS.

Rebels at home! go hide your faces—
　Weep for your crimes with bitter tears;
You could not bind the blessed daylight,
　Though you should strive a thousand years!—CHORUS.

Back to your dens, ye secret traitors!
　Down to your own degraded spheres!
Ere the first blaze of dazzling sunshine
　Shortens your lives a thousand years.—CHORUS.

Haste thee along, thou glorious Noonday!
　Oh, for the eyes of ancient seers!
Oh, for the faith of Him who reckons
　Each of His days a thousand years!—CHORUS.

THE SOLDIER TRAMP.

Scene—A City Police Court.

"Yer honor, I pleads guilty; I'm a bummer;
  I don't deny the cop here found me drunk;
I don't deny that through the whole. long summer,
  The sun warmed earth has been my only bunk.
I hain't been able fur to earn a livin';
  A man with one leg planted in the tomb
Can't git a job—an' I've a strong misgivin'
  'Bout bein' cooped up in a Soldiers' Home.

" 'Whar did I lose my leg?' At Spottsylvania—
  Perhaps you've read about the bloody fight—
But then I guess the story won't restrain you
  From doin' what the law sets down as right.
I'm not a vag through choice, but through misfortune,
  An' as fur drink—well, all men have there faults;
An', judge, I guess I've had my lawful portion
  O' rough experiences in prison vaults.

"I served as a private in the Tenth New Jersey,
  An' all the boys'll say I done what's right;
Thar ain't a man kin say that Abram Bursey
  War ever found a-shirkin' in a fight.
Right in the hell-born, frightful roar o' battle,
  Whar shot an' shell shrieked thro' the darksome wood,
And where the minnie balls like hail did rattle,
  You'd always find me doin' the best I could.

"We had a brave ol' feller for a Colonel—
  We called him Sweety, but his name was Sweet—
Why, judge; I swar it, by the Great Eternal!
  That brave ol' cuss 'd rather fight than eat.
An' you could allus bet your bottom dollar
  In battle, Sweety 'd never hunt a tree;
He'd allus push into the front an' holler:
  'Brace up, my gallant boys, an' follow me!'

"Well, jest afore the Spottsylvania battle,
  Ol' Sweety cum to me an' says, says he:
'I tell you Abe, 'taint many things 'll rattle
  A tough, old, weather-beaten cuss like me;
But in my very soul I've got a feelin'
  That I'm goin' to get a dose to-day,
An' 'taint no use fur me to be concealin'
  The skittish thoughts that in my bosom play.

"Fur many years you've been my neighbor, Bursey,
  An' I hev allus found you squar and true—
Back in our little town in old New Jersey
  No one has got a better name than you.

An' now I want yer promise, squar'ly given,
　　That if our cause to-day demands my life,
An' you yourself are left among the livin',
　　You'll take me back an' lay me by my wife." ,

"Well, judge, that day, amidst the most infernal
　　An' desp'rate bloody fight I ever seed,
'Way up in front I saw the brave ol' Colonel
　　Throw up his hands and tumble off his steed.
In half a minute I was bending o'er him,
　　An' seein' that he wasn't killed outright,
I loaded him up on my back an' bore him
　　Some little distance back out o' the fight.

"The blood from out a ghastly wound was flowin',
　　An' so I snatched the shirt from off my back,
For I could see the brave ol' cuss war goin'
　　To die, unless I held the red tide back.
An' purty soon I seed he was revivin',
　　An' heard him whisper: 'Abe, you've saved my life,
Your ol' wool shirt, along with your connivin',
　　Has kept me from that grave beside my wife.'

"Well, judge, while I stood thar beside him, schemin'
　　On how to get him in a doctor's care,
A ten-pound shell, toward us come a screamin'
　　Just like a ravin' demon in the air.
An' w'en it passed, I found myself a lyin'
　　Across ol' Sweety's body, an' I see
That 'tarnal shell, that by us went a flyin'
　　Had tuk my leg along fur company.

"Well, judge, that's all; 'cept when the war was over,
　　I found myself a cripple, an' since then
I've been a sort o' shiftless, worthless rover,
　　But jest as honest as the most o' men.
I never stole a dime from livin' mortal,
　　Nor ever harmed a woman, child or man—
I've simply been a bum, and hope the court'll
　　Be jest as easy on me as it can.

Then spake the judge: "Such helpless, worthless creatures
　　Should never be allowed to bum and beg;
Your case, 'tis true, has some redeeming features,
　　For in your country's cause you lost a leg.
And yet I feel the world needs an example
　　To check the tendency of men to roam;
The sentence is, That all your life—your camp'll
　　Be in the best room in my humble home."

The soldier stared! Dumb! 'Silent as a statue!
   Then, in a voice of trembling pathos, said:
"Judge, turn your head, and give me one look at you—
   That voice is like an echo from the dead."
Then forward limped he, grimy hand extended,
   While tears adown his sun-brown cheeks did roll,
And said, with slang and pathos strangely blended:
   "Why, Colonel Sweety, durn your brave ol' soul."
—*Dan Santiago Caroline.*

THE CRUTCH IN THE CORNER.

[Written just after the war by John McIntosh—"Old Vermont"].

"Why. Billy, your room is as cold as the hut
   We had by the swamp and river,
Where we lost our Major, and Tim, you know,
   And sixty more with the fever."
"Well, Tom. old fellow, it's hard enough,
   But the best at times knock under;
There's ne'er a stick of wood in the house
   But that crutch in the corner yonder!

"Sorry I listed? Don't ask me that, Tom;
   If the flag was again in danger,
I'd aim the gun with an aching stump
   At the foe, were he brother or stranger.
But, I say, ought a wound from a shot or shell,
   Or a pistol bullet, by thunder!
Forever doom a poor fellow to want,
   With that crutch in the corner yonder?

"That crutch, old comrade, ought ever to be
   A draft at sight on the Nation,
For honor, respect, and a friendly hand,
   For clothing, and quarters, and rations!
My wife—she begs at the Nugget House,
   Where the bigbugs live in splendor,
And brag o'er the wine, of the fights that brought
   Such as that in the corner yonder!

"And Charlie—he goes to some place up town
   Some ticket-for-soup arrangement;
All well enough for a hungry boy,
   But. Tom, its effect is estrangement;
I'd sooner have kicked the bucket twice o'er,
   By a shell or a round ten-pounder,
Than live such a life as I'm doing now,
   With that crutch in the corner yonder.

"There's ne'er a thing left to pawn or to sell,
    And the winter has closed on labor;
This medal is all that is left me now,
    With my pistols and trusty saber;
And those, by the sunlight above us, Tom,
    No power from my trust shall sunder,
Save the One that releases me at last
    From that crutch in the corner yonder.

"I can raise this arm that is left to me
    To the blessed heaven above us,
And swear by the throne of the Father there,
    And the angels all, who love us,
That the hand I lost and the hand I have
    Were never yet stained by plunder,
And, for love of the dear old flag, I now
    Use that crutch in the corner yonder.

"Do I ask too much when I say we boys
    Who fought for the Nation's glory,
Now that the danger is past and gone,
    In comfort should tell our story?
How would we have fought when the mad shells screamed
    And shivered our ranks, I wonder,
Had we known our lot would have been to beg,
    With that crutch in the corner yonder?

"There's little we hear of nowadays
    But pardon and reconstruction,
While the soldier who fought and bled for both
    Is left to his own destruction.
'Twould be well, I think, in these nipping times,
    For those Congress fellows to ponder,
And think of us boys who use such things
    As that crutch in the corner yonder."

THE STAR SPANGLED BANNER.

BY FRANCIS H. KEY.

Oh say can you see by the dawn's early light,
    What so proudly we hail'd at the twilight's last gleaming?
Whose broad stripes and bright stars thro' the perilous fight,
    O'er the ramparts we watch'd were so gallantly streaming!
And the rocket's red glare, the bombs bursting in air,
    Gave proof through the night that our flag was still there.

CHORUS.

Oh say, does the star spangled banner yet wave,
    O'er the land of the free and the home of the brave?

On the shore dimly seen thro' the mist of the deep,
Where the foe's haughty host in dread silence reposes,
What is that which the breeze, o'er the towering steep,
As it fitfully blows, half conceals, half discloses?
Now it catches the gleam of the morning's first beam,
In full glory reflected now shines in the stream.

CHORUS.

'Tis the Star Spangled Banner! O long may it wave,
O'er the land, etc., etc.

And where is that band who so vauntingly swore,
That the havoc of war and the battle's confusion,
A home and a country should leave us no more?
Their blood has wash'd out their foul footsteps' pollution.
No refuge could save the hirelings and slave,
From the terror of flight or the gloom of the grave.

CHORUS.

. And the Star Spangled Banner in triumph doth wave,
O'er the land, etc., etc.

Oh thus be it ever, when freemen shall stand
Between their loved home and the war's desolation;
Blest with vict'ry and peace, may the heav'n rescued land
Praise the Power that hath made and preserv'd us a nation,
Then conquer we must, when our cause it is just,
And this be our motto, "In God is our trust."

CHORUS.

And the Star Spangled Banner forever shall wave,
O'er the land, etc., etc.

THE SWORD OF BUNKER HILL.

KEY OF A.

He lay upon his dying bed,
His eye was growing dim,
· When with a feeble voice he called
His weeping son to him:
"Weep not, my boy," the veteran said,
"I bow to Heaven's high will,
But quickly from yon antlers bring   } REPEAT.
The sword of Bunker Hill."

The sword was brought, the soldier's eye
Lit with a sudden flame;
And as he grasp'd the ancient blade,
He murmur'd Warren's name;

Then said, "My boy, I leave you gold,
  But what is richer still,
I leave you, mark me, mark me now,
  The sword of Bunker Hill." } REPEAT.

" 'Twas on that dread, immortal day,
  I dared the Briton's band,
A captain raised this blade on me,
  I tore it from his hand;
And while the glorious battle raged,
  It lighten'd Freedom's will,
For, boy, the God of Freedom bless'd
  The sword of Bunker Hill." } REPEAT.

'Oh! keep the sword,"—his accents broke,
  A smile and he was dead;
But his wrinkled hand still grasp'd the blade,
  Upon that dying bed.
The son remains, the sword remains,
  Its glory growing still,
And sixty millions bless'd the sire
  And sword of Bunker Hill. } REPEAT.

COLUMBIA, THE GEM OF THE OCEAN.

OR RED, WHITE AND BLUE—KEY OF G.

O Columbia! the gem of the ocean,
  The home of the brave and the free,
The shrine of each patriot's devotion,
  A World offers homage to thee.
The mandates make heroes assemble,
  When Liberty's form stands in view;
Thy banners make tyranny tremble,
  When borne by the red, white and blue.

CHORUS—When borne by the red, white and blue,
      When borne by the red, white and blue,
      Thy banners make tyranny tremble,
      When borne by the red, white and blue.

When war waged its wide desolation,
  And threatened the land to deform,
The ark then of freedom's foundation,—
  Columbia—rode safe through the storm;
With her garlands of vict'ry around her,
  When so proudly she bore her brave crew.
With her flag proudly floating before her,
  The boast of the red, white and blue.—CHORUS.

That banner, that banner, bring hither,
    Tho' rebels and traitors look grim;
May the wreaths it has won never wither,
    Nor the stars of Its glory grow dim!
May the service united ne'er sever,
    But they to their colors prove true!
The Army and Navy forever,
    Three cheers for the red, white and blue.—CHORUS.

THE LOYAL "DIXIE."

[Written in 1865, to be *sung* in lieu of the Rebel "Dixie" which, just at that time, was supposed to be pretty badly "played"].

BY "JARGO NETHLIZ."

When Jeff's rebellion first begun
The rebels thought 'twould just be "fun"
And "play" to slay our loyal Union band.
And just to cheer their boys along
They used to sing that little song
Called "Away, away, away in "Dixie's Land."

CHORUS—But now the people do demand
          "Ropes!" "Ropes!"
To hang the leaders of this band
And make all traitors understand
That they must pay "*the penalty of treason.*"

At first we tried with all our might
To compromise. and save a fight,
But they said "Nay, your offers we decline,"
So when no other course would save us,
We gave them a thrashing, and caught Jeff Davis
Hid away, away, beneath a "*crinoline.*"

CHORUS—And now the people do demand, &c.

And now the soldiers want to know
Will Uncle Sam let traitors go
Away. away, unpunished for this crime?
If *we* were "bossing" these affairs
We'd counsel them to *say their prayers*
Right away, right away, or they might be short of time.

CHORUS—For now the people, &c.

THE ARMY BEAN, No. 1.

Air.—"Sweet By and By."

There's a spot that the soldiers all love,
  The mess-tent is the place that we mean;
And the dish that we like to see there,
  Is the old-fashioned, white Army bean.

CHORUS—'Tis the bean that we mean,
        And we'll eat as we ne'r ate before;
      The Army bean, nice and clean;
        We will stick to our beans evermore.

Now the bean in its primitive state,
  Is a plant we have all often met;
And when cooked in the old army style,
  It has charms we can never forget.—CHORUS.

The German is fond of saur kraut,
  The potato is loved by the Mick;
But the soldiers have long since found out,
  That thro' life to our beans we should stick.—CHORUS.

REFRAIN—Air—"Tell Aunt Rhoda."
        Beans for breakfast,
        Beans for dinner,
        Beans for supper,
        Beans! Beans!! Beans!!!

ODES OF THE G. A. R.

AULD LANG SYNE.

BY ROBERT BURNS.

Should auld acquaintance be forgot
  And never brought to mind?
Should auld acquaintance be forgot,
  And days of auld lang syne?

We twa hae run about the braes
  And pu'd the gowans fine;
But we've wander'd many a weary foot
  Sin' auld lang syne.

We too hae paddled i' the burn
  Frae morning sun till dine;
But seas between us braid ha'e roar'd
  Sin' auld lang syne.

And there's a hand, my trusty friend,
  And gie 's a hand o' thine;
And we'll tak' a right gude willie waught
  For auld lang syne.

And surely you'll be your pint stoup,
  And surely I'll be mine;
And we'll take a cup o' kindness yet
  For auld lang syne.

CHARITY.

Air—Nettleton—"Come Thou Fount."

Meek and lowly, pure and holy,
  Chief among the "blessed three,"
Turning sadness into gladness,
  Heaven-born art thou, Charity!
Pity dwel'eth in thy bosom,
  Kindness reigneth o'er thy heart,
Gentle thoughts alone can sway thee,
  Judgment hath in thee no part.

Meek and lowly, pure and holy,
  Chief among the "blessed three,"
Turning sadness into gladness,
  Heaven-born art thou, Charity!
Hoping ever, failing never,
  Though deceived, believing still;
Long abiding, all confiding
  To thy heavenly Father's will.

Never weary of well-doing,
  Never fearful of the end;
' Claiming all mankind as brothers,
  Thou dost all alike befriend.
Meek and lowly, pure and holy,
  Chief among the "blessed three,'
Turning sadness into gladness,
  Heaven-born art thou, Charity!

AMERICA.

My country, 'tis of thee,
Sweet land of liberty,
  Of thee I sing!
Land where my fathers died,
Land of the pilgrims' pride,
From ev'ry mountain-side
  Let freedom ring!

My native country, thee,
Land of the noble free,
  Thy name I love;
I love thy rocks and rills,
Thy woods and templed hills:
My heart with rapture thrills,
  Like that above.

Let music swell the breeze,
And ring from all the trees
  Sweet freedom's song;
Let mortal tongues awake,
Let all that breathe partake,
Let rocks their silence break,
  The sound prolong.

Our fathers' God! to thee,
Author of liberty,
  To thee we sing.
Long may our land be bright
With freedom's holy light;
Protect us by thy might,
  Great God, our King!

THE G. A. R. AND W. R. C. "RELIEF SONG."

THE COTTAGE OF THE DEAR ONES LEFT AT HOME.*

[Dedicated to the memory of Gov. O. P. Morton. "War Governor" of Indiana, by Major J. H. Lozier, of his Official Staff.]

I have oft been standing where our boys were marching
  Along their hot and dusty road;
While, with thirst and with fever their pale lips were parching,
  And their proud forms trembled 'neath their load.
But though they were feeble and foot sore and weary,
  They still marched steadily along;
And their spirits were light and their voices were merry,
  As they marched to the music of their song.
   *See page 14,

CHORUS.

O, while the loved ones weep for those who lowly sleep
  Within the soldiers' honored tomb,
Let want fall lightly, and the fire burn brightly,
  In the cottage of the dear ones left at home.

I have stood on the field where the red tide of battle,
  Was wildly dashing to and fro;
And the death-dealing cannon and fierce muskets' rattle
  Was laying many heroes low.
But the soldier stood firm to the duty before him,
  Nor heeded the cannon's deadly boom;
But he thought of the Being who still hovered o'er him,
  And the cottage of the dear ones left at home.

I have stood by the cot where the soldier was lying,
  And oft times closed his dying eyes;
And it is not the grave, nor the terror of dying,
  That troubles the soldier when he dies.
But he fears that the world, in its chase after pleasures,
  Will not stop to look upon life's gloom;
And that none but the Master will care for his treasures
  In the cottage of the dear ones left at home.

ODES OF THE W. R. C.

OPENING ODE.

Air—"Keller's American Hymn."

Bright o'er our country the sunshine of Peace
Smiles where the war-cloud long darkened the air—

Long may it smile o'er a prosperous land—
While we assemble our brothers to aid,
 And in their labors of charity share!

REPEAT—Long may it smile, etc.

Cold now are firesides, with love once aglow,
 Cold are brave hearts that for us nobly fought!
Loved ones they left, 'tis our task now to cheer,
Help we the helpless in sorrow who bow,
 Comfort we bring where was misery brought!

REPEAT—Loved ones they left, etc.

Land that we love best, dear land of our birth!
 Land twice redeemed by the blood of the brave,—
God in his wisdom protect thee alway!
Onward thy progress in honor and worth,
 Aye, may thy starry flag over thee wave.

REPEAT—God in his wisdom, etc.

CHAPLAIN LOZIER'S VERSION OF THE FOREGOING OPENING ODE OF THE W. R. C.*

AIR.—"What a Friend we have in Jesus.

Bright above our prosp'rous Nation,
 Shines the glorious Sun of Peace,
Stretching forth its "Bow of Promise,"—
 —Pledge that *Treason's* storm shall cease!
May its smile abide forever,
 Where War clouded once the air,—
—While we meet to aid our Brothers,
 And their "*Works of Love*" to share.

Cold are firesides now,—once glowing;
 Cold are hearts that nobly fought,
Come we now, our help bestowing,
 Where these Missing ones are not.
Help we helpless ones in sorrow,
 Cheer we hearts o'erwhelmed with care,—
—While we meet to aid our Brothers,
 And their "*Works of Love*" to share.

Native Land! God speed thee onward!
 Twice redeemed by Patriots' blood ;
All our loyal hearts commend thee
 To the keeping care of God.
May our Starry Banner ever
 Hallow, with its folds, the air,—
—While we meet to aid our Brothers,
 And their "*Works of Love*" to share.

*NOTE.—"Keller's American Hymn" being difficult to sing without the music in hand, at the request of leading officers of the W. R. C., Chaplain Lozier has paraphrased the words of the old ode, adapting them to a *familiar* tune which all can readily sing.

INITIATION ODE.

Air—Webb—"From Greenland's Icy Mountains."

With warm and kindly greeting,
　　We gladly welcome you;
Each heart responsive beating,
　　In friendship tried and true.
A high and noble purpose,
　　Moves every heart and hand;
We work for those whose valor,
　　From treason saved our land.

For those, alas! whose numbers
　　Grow less each passing year;
For those who fought to save us
　　The homes we hold so dear.
We work for those brave martyrs,
　　The army of the slain;
Whose nameless graves are scattered
　　O'er many a Southern plain.

For widowed ones and orphans,
　　Left to our loving care;
Our hands will gladly labor,
　　Our hearts their sorrows share.
Then once more kindly greeting,
　　And welcome we extend;
May each and all prove worthy
　　To be the soldiers' friend.

ODES OF THE S. OF V.

OPENING HYMN.

[At command, ATTENTION, after the opening prayer.]

Air—"America."

God bless our native land!
Firm may she ever stand,
　　Through storm and night;
When the wild tempests rave
Ruler of wind and wave,
Do thou our country save
　　By thy great might.

MUSTER HYMN.

[After the obligation is delivered to Recruits, and the Chaplain's prayer is completed, at the command, CAMP, ATTENTION ! Sing the following:]

Air.—" Sweet bye and bye."

Firm, united in our noble cause,
Loyal Brothers together we stand,
Friendship, Charity and Loyalty our laws;
We will spread them all over our land.
We will fight for the right,
And the memories of heroes gone before.
Ever blest the glorious light
Of freedom, blood-stained but secure.

CLOSING HYMN.

[At the command, ATTENTION! after the Chaplain's closing prayer sing:

Air.—" Greenville."

(Popularly known as " Days of Absence," and " Come ye Sinners poor and needy.")

Brothers, now our work completed
Let us to our homes repair,
Still to friendship dedicated,
We will each perform our share.
Let our charity be abounding,
Unto all who wore the blue,
And in loyalty united,
We will to our land be true.

Bearing high the noble banner,
Stained with blood of patriot sires,
We will ever on our altars,
Keep alive fair freedom's fires.
And the memories ever precious,
Of the heroes gone before,
As Sons of Veterans, we will cherish
Until time shall be no more.

INDEX.

40

ROUNDS

FROM THE CARTRIDGE BOX OF THE

Fighting  Chaplain

EMBRACING THE "CREAM" OF THE "OLD WAR SONGS" AND RECITATIONS,
AND THE ODES OF THE

W. R. C.

G. A. R. S. of V.

PRICE 25 CTS

Per Dozen to Posts, Camps, Corps or Agents, at the rate of 15 Cents Each, Post Paid.

www.ingramcontent.com/pod-product-compliance
Lightning Source LLC
Chambersburg PA
CBHW031746090426
42739CB00008B/896